SEEING RED

Taylor Swift

Mary Boone

This book is available in quantity at special discounts for your group or organization. For further information, contact:

Triumph Books LLC
814 North Franklin Street
Chicago, Illinois 60610
Phone: (312) 337-0747
www.triumphbooks.com

Printed in U.S.A.

ISBN: 978-1-60078-902-1

Content developed and packaged by Rockett Media, Inc.
Writer: Mary Boone
Editor: Bob Baker
Design: Andrew Burwell
Page Production: Chad Bell
Cover Design by Andrew Burwell

Photographs courtesy of Getty Images unless otherwise noted.

SEEING RED
Taylor Swift

From Pennsylvania to Nashville to the World

Chapter 1:
FROM PENNSYLVANIA TO NASHVILLE TO THE WORLD

Back in 2006, a new-to-the-scene Taylor Swift told an Associated Press reporter she wasn't scared of the sometimes rough-and-tumble country music industry.

"Not by any measure," she said. "I'm intimidated by the fear of being average."

Average?

When searching for words to describe Taylor, "average" hardly ever comes into play. Writers have called her "beautiful," "prodigy," "quirky" and "genuine" – but not average.

Average kids don't start writing songs while they're still in kindergarten. They don't, at age 11, perform the national anthem at a Philadelphia 76ers game or show up at record company offices announcing they want a record deal. And then, when they get that deal at age 13, they certainly don't back out of their contract because they don't want to sing other writers' songs.

Taylor Alison Swift is a lot of things, but average isn't one of them.

Taylor grew up on a Christmas tree farm in southeastern Pennsylvania and got her love of music from her maternal grandmother, Marjorie Finlay, an opera singer.

"I can remember her singing," Taylor told her hometown newspaper in 2008. "She

Taylor's all dressed up for the 2010 Nashville Symphony Ball.

THE TAYLOR FILE

Full name: Taylor Alison Swift
Parents: Scott and Andrea Swift
Siblings: Younger brother, Austin
Birthdate: Dec. 13, 1989
Music label: Big Machine
Her band: The Agency
In the bank: She's No. 3 on Forbes' 2012 list of the nation's highest-paid female entertainers (behind only Oprah Winfrey and Britney Spears). According to the magazine, Taylor earned an estimated $57 million between May 2011 and May 2012.
Website: www.taylorswift.com
Twitter: @taylorswift13

Taylor Swift performs in Kansas City .

Taylor at the 2006 Country Music Awards.

MEETING TIM MCGRAW

Taylor Swift wrote her first hit single, "Tim McGraw," long before she met the handsome country singer.

"The idea for this song came to me in math class. I just started singing to myself 'When you think Tim McGraw.' The concept for this song hit me, because I was dating a guy who moved away, and it was going to be over for us. So I started thinking of things that I knew would remind him of me," Taylor told Fanpop.com. "The first thing that came to mind was that my favorite song is by Tim McGraw. After school, I went downtown, sat down at the piano, and wrote this with Liz Rose in fifteen minutes. It may be the best fifteen minutes I've ever experienced."

The song was released on June 19, 2006, by Big Machine Records as the lead single from Taylor's self-titled debut album, *Taylor Swift*.

Eleven months later, at the 2007 Academy of Country Music Awards, Taylor finally got to meet the inspiration for her hit. While singing "Tim McGraw," Taylor boldly walked into the audience and stopped right in front of Tim. At the end of the song, she shook hands with the singer and said, "Hi, I'm Taylor."

McGraw, who has won 3 Grammys, 14 Academy of Country Music awards, 11 Country Music Association (CMA) awards, 10 American Music Awards, and 3 People's Choice Awards, was flattered by Taylor's lyrics.

The young singer figured it wouldn't hurt to ask about the possibility of opening a series of shows on Tim's upcoming tour with his wife, Faith Hill. She

MEETING TIM MCGRAW (CONT.)

told Dial-Global about hitting him up for a spot on the show:

"I asked him, 'How come you don't take opening acts out on the Soul2Soul tour?' And he asked, 'Why? Do you have someone in mind?' I said, 'Yeah, I do. She sings a song with your name as the title.' I was like, 'I'd love to be on tour with you if you have any extra time before your show.' I definitely was a little bit outgoing in that sense."

It seems her self-confidence paid off: She joined the Soul2Soul tour for a handful of dates in summer 2007.

But that wasn't the end of the Taylor-Tim connection.

Taylor joins McGraw in a duet on his 2013 album *Two Lanes of Freedom*. Taylor and McGraw team up on the single "Highway Don't Care," which also features Keith Urban on guitar.

"Taylor is really special," McGraw told CMT Radio, "and she's gotten exponentially better with every project. She owns her style now. Instead of searching for a style or trying to be something, she owns who she is."

Faith Hill and Tim McGraw present Taylor with the 2009 Country Music Association Entertainer of the Year Award.

Taylor and Tim McGraw attend a women's cancer benefit in 2010.

was one of my first inspirations."

As a kid Taylor loved to write poetry and songs, often using the exercise as a means of working through feelings of being left out or overlooked at school.

"I love words," Taylor told the *Reading (Penn.) Eagle*. "I love to write. Being an artist is what I love."

The Swift family regularly made the two-and-a-half-hour trip from their home in Wyomissing, Penn., to New York City to attend Broadway performances and for singing and acting lessons. While still in elementary school, Taylor became smitten with musical theater. After a few years of auditions and not getting any roles, however, she turned her attention to country music and began dreaming of becoming a songwriter. The pre-teen performed anywhere she could find an audience: local festivals and fairs, garden club meetings and hospitals.

"I've never felt like the coolest girl in the room. Ever."

*– **Taylor Swift** to People magazine, 2012*

When she was 11, Taylor won a local talent contest. The prize was the

Taylor at the 2012 Academy of Country Music Awards.

Taylor sings the national anthem at a 2006 NFL matchup between the Miami Dolphins and the Detroit Lions.

COLLABORATOR: *LIZ ROSE*

When Taylor Swift first found success as a teenager singing about high school crushes, friendship and fitting in, her unlikely – but successful — co-writer was a middle-aged mother of three: Liz Rose.

Rose may not have been going through the same experiences Taylor was, but she knew how to help the young singer get the words out.

Rose moved from Texas to Nashville in 1994. The stay-at-home mom divorced shortly after the move and had to jump back into the workforce. She had a series of jobs in the music industry, including marketing, publishing, management and working for country crooners Brooks & Dunn. Along the way, she found ways to help struggling songwriters.

"I'm not an artist and I don't play, so I never tried to write Liz Rose songs," she told Broadcast Music Inc. in 2011. "I was just trying to get with these amazing people and pull out of them what they did best."

And help she did. During those early years, Rose's songs were recorded by singers including Tim McGraw, Billy Gilman, Trisha Yearwood, Martina McBride, Jewel, Bonnie Raitt and Gary Allan.

Then, Rose started working with Taylor. It was a match made in heaven.

"I think she ended up just writing with me because I didn't change what she was doing," Rose told American Songwriter in 2010. "I tried to make it better and mold it and hone it, and hang on there and write it down; that's why it worked with us. I really respected and got what she was trying to do, and I didn't want to make her write in the Nashville cookie-cutter songwriting mold.

"I remember her coming in and saying, 'I wanna write a song called "When You Think Tim McGraw,"' and the first thing that went through my mind was, 'Okay, we're gonna write this song, and you don't have a record deal, and nobody else is gonna cut it,'" Rose recalls. "I said, 'Okay! I'm not gonna argue!'"

The two collaborated on seven songs on Taylor's self-titled debut album; one of those songs was the hit single "Tim McGraw."

"I love writing with Liz," Taylor told Songwriter Universe in 2007. "When we write, I usually come in with a melody and some lyric content, and then we'll work on creating the rest of the song. She's a really good song editor."

Taylor and Rose have teamed up on more than a dozen songs, including "Picture To Burn," "Fearless" and "You Belong With Me." They also co-wrote "Teardrops on My Guitar," which helped Rose win the 2007 Songwriter of the Year award from SESAC and "White Horse," which won a Grammy Award in 2010.

Even as Taylor has grown as a songwriter, she continues to seek out Rose's talents. The two co-wrote "All Too Well" on Taylor's new album, *Red*.

In 2010, Rose started her own publishing company, Liz Rose Music, Inc. The business is focused on signing uniquely talented and driven writers.

One of Rose's own children is also a singer/songwriter. Caitlin Rose's first album, *Own Side Now*, was released by Names Records in 2010.

Taylor and Liz Rose pick up a 2010 Grammy Award for "White Horse."

Chapter 1:
FROM PENNSYLVANIA TO NASHVILLE TO THE WORLD

opportunity to appear as the opening act for country rock star Charlie Daniels' Strausstown, Penn., show. For Taylor, this was a step toward achieving her dreams but it was just a tiny step. She was certain success could not be hers until she traveled to Nashville.

And so she did.

"'I took my demo CDs of karaoke songs, where I sound like a chipmunk – it's pretty awesome – to Nashville, and my mom waited in the car while I knocked on doors up and down Music Row," she told *Entertainment Weekly* in 2008. "I would say, 'Hi, I'm Taylor. I'm 11. I want a record deal. Call me.'"

Undaunted by the dozens of rejections she received, Taylor set out to grow and improve. She learned to play the guitar and began to focus more on songwriting. And her family, fully supporting her devotion to her art, relocated to the Nashville suburb of Hendersonville.

In 2004, at age 14, Taylor began working with a New York talent agency. A year later, her family dumped the agent but not before taking some meetings with Nashville's major record labels. After performing at an RCA Records showcase, the eighth-grader was given a development deal.

Taylor had been working for years to get a record deal, so it was an especially difficult decision for the teen to nix the contract when RCA insisted she sing other writers' songs. Around that same time, she became the youngest songwriter to sign a publishing deal with Sony - with the specification that she didn't want her songs sung by other artists. She was young but she knew exactly where she wanted to end up and how she wanted to get there.

Music industry veteran Scott Borchetta met Taylor just after her RCA deal fell apart and says he was struck by her "real inner vision."

"She played some songs in our first meeting and I was just killed on sight," Borchetta told the *Boston Globe* in 2008. "She's the full package, somebody who writes her own songs, and is so good at

TAYLOR SWIFT
THE ALBUM

Taylor's debut, self-titled album was released in October 2006 by Big Machine Records. The album topped the Country Albums chart for 24 consecutive weeks. By the end of 2012, Taylor Swift *had logged 269 weeks on the Billboard Top 200/Pop Albums chart, making it one of the 12 longest-running albums in the chart's 57-year history. The album tracks are:*

"A Place In This World"
"Cold As You"
"Mary's Song (Oh My My My)"
"Our Song"
"Picture to Burn"
"Should've Said No"
"Stay Beautiful"
"Teardrops On My Guitar"
"The Outside"
"Tied Together With A Smile"
"Tim McGraw"

Taylor is all glammed up as she arrives at the 2006 Country Music Association Awards.

Taylor was among the honorees at the 2011 CMT Artists of the Year Celebration in Nashville.

it, so smart; who sings, plays the guitar, looks as good as she looks, works that hard, is that engaging and so savvy. It's an extraordinary combination."

Borchetta was planning a new label, Big Machine Records, at the time and was thrilled to land Swift as its centerpiece.

While former classmates were focused on football games, shopping and school dances, Taylor began home-schooling so she could focus even more intensely on her music.

Her self-titled debut was released when she was 16 years old. She wrote all 11 songs on the album. "Our Song," her third single, became a gigantic hit and made her the youngest person ever to both write and perform a No. 1 song on the country charts. She received a Best New Artist nomination at the 2008 Grammy Awards.

Her second album, *Fearless*, became the top-selling album of 2009 and won four Grammy Awards. Taylor's third album, 2010's *Speak Now*, sold more than 1 million copies in its first week of release in the United States; one of the singles from the album, "Mean," won two Grammys.

Her current album, *Red*, was released Oct. 22, 2012, and had first week U.S. sales of 1.21 million. The album also topped international sales charts in the United Kingdom, Ireland, Canada, Brazil, Argentina, Mexico, Japan, Malaysia, Australia and New Zealand. Taylor's become a cover girl for magazines ranging from *Rolling Stone* to *Seventeen*. She has performed with legends of the pop, rock, country and even rap world. In the past half-dozen years, she's collected more Grammys, Country Music Awards and American Music Awards than most acts amass in a lifetime.

Average? Not by a long shot, Miss Swift. Set aside your fears. You are, in fact, quite extraordinary.

"I write songs about my life: it's not something I've kept secret and pretty much everyone knows that, so no, I don't worry that a new man will get upset about something I write. That being said, it's mind-blowing how some guys have just handed me inspiration for some of these songs on a plate."

– **Taylor Swift** *to the* London Daily Mail, *2012*

SOUNDTRACKS, SEUSS AND CSI

As if selling a bazillion albums wasn't enough, Taylor Swift has been testing her acting chops.

Taylor's first real acting gig came when she appeared in the music video for Brad Paisley's song "Online." The satiric view of social networking sites won a Video of the Year award for Paisley at the 2007 Country Music Association awards.

In 2008 she helped MTV film a documentary, and in the same year joined the Jonas Brothers in their 3D concert film that earned more than $12.7 million in its opening weekend.

In March 2009, Taylor made her TV acting debut when she appeared as a young crime victim on the *CSI* episode called "Turn, Turn, Turn." She has also made appearances in *Hannah Montana the Movie*, and Kellie Pickler's music video "Best Days of Your Life."

More recently, the Nashville beauty voiced a character for the animated movie *The Lorax* and appeared with then-boyfriend Taylor Lautner in the 2010 romantic comedy *Valentine's Day*.

Taylor says when she first started out, she was hoping for a career in acting, not music.

"I went to several auditions in New York. I was always going there for vocal and acting lessons ... and for auditions, where you stand in line in a long hallway with a lot of people," she told Tasteofcountry.com. "After a few years of auditioning in New York and not getting anything, I started writing songs. But I never lost my love for theater."

Now that's she's dipped her toe into the acting pool, Taylor says she might someday consider bigger roles on the big screen.

"I would love to sign on to do a movie if it was the right role and if it was the right script, because I would be taking time away from music to tell a big grand story, and spend all of my time and pouring all of my emotions into being someone else," she told *Time* magazine in 2012. "So, for me to do that, it would have to be a story worth telling."

Apparently one of the tales Taylor thinks may be worth telling is the story of singer Joni Mitchell's life. It's been rumored that Taylor will play the Canadian songstress in an upcoming film.

"I wish I could say it's confirmed," she told *Time*. "But the thing about movies that I've learned is – I've been reading scripts for five years, and you just don't know which ones are going to get greenlit and which ones aren't, so I can't talk about it unless it's the real thing."

Taylor attends the Hollywood premiere of *The Lorax*.

Chapter 2:

Overachiever

Chapter 2:
OVERACHIEVER

Biggest, brightest, youngest, most talented, cutest in polka dots. It's virtually impossible to describe Taylor Swift without using at least a handful of superlatives.

From the very beginning of her career, Taylor's determination and talent have combined to exceed expectations. Her extraordinary voice and relatable lyrics have earned the young singer a number of mentions in the music record books.

Taylor insists she didn't set out with the goal to get more radio play than Carrie Underwood or sell more concert tickets than Miranda Lambert. Instead, she's got an inner need to succeed – a one-woman race to win.

"I've always approached this from the place where I don't compete with other girls," she told *Dateline NBC* in 2009. "I don't compete with other people in the industry, I compete with myself. If I looked at every other girl in the entertainment industry as competition, my life would be

Taylor makes a big haul at the 2012 MTV Europe Music Awards.

Taylor was a six-time winner at the 2011 Teen Choice Awards.

BANJO MOJO

Traditional banjos have four or five strings. Keen observers, however, will notice that Taylor Swift is among a growing number of musicians who prefer to play a six-string banjo.

The folks at Deering banjo company say the banjo is experiencing a real renaissance. More and more folks are coming to banjo for the first time or are returning to it after many years. Some of the interest is coming from guitar-playing musicians who want to expand their musical repertoire. Many of them would like to take their existing skill set and transfer it to the banjo – which is easiest to do on a six string banjo.

The six-string has been around for decades but it's enjoying an upsurge in popularity thanks to artists including Taylor Swift, Keith Urban, Joe Satriani, Taj Mahal and John Fogerty.

Taylor plays a Deering Boston Acoustic/Electric Six-String Banjo on her 2012 hit "Mean." The instrument's manufacturer says it has big, resonant bass and crisp high notes not found on a five-string.

In addition to the banjo, Taylor plays guitar, piano and ukulele.

The song "Mean" earned Taylor two Grammys in 2012, one for Best Country Song and another for Best Country Solo Performance.

Every time she hears her name called at an awards show, Taylor insists the surprise is real. Here, she accepts in 2011 American Music Award for Favorite Country Female Artist.

really lonely."

It seems Taylor is the only competition Taylor needs.

Guided by her personal pursuit of perfection, the young songstress has enjoyed more success in six years than most entertainers could hope for in six decades. Among some of her more notable achievements:

Youngest

Faith Hill was 26 years old when her debut album was released. Brad Paisley and Blake Shelton were 27 and 25, respectively, when their first albums came out. The fact that Taylor got into the business so young – she was 17 when her self-titled debut was released – means she got a bit of a head start on many of her fellow musicians.

At age 14, she became the youngest songwriter ever hired by the Sony/ATV Music publishing house.

In 2008, Taylor became the youngest solo artist ever to top year-end album sales charts with her album *Fearless*.

In 2009, at age 19, Taylor beat out some of the biggest names in country to become the youngest person ever

"I'm a really big worrier. I can't believe I get to have the life I have, so I've got a complete fear of messing up, of making a misstep where it all comes crumbling down. It's a high-wire act in my brain all the time."
– ***Taylor Swift*** *to the*
London Daily Mail, 2012

Taylor wins a 2013 People's Choice Award as Favorite Country Artist.

to win the Country Music Association's Entertainer of the Year Award. She also was the youngest artist to win Album of the Year honors from the Academy of Country Music

In 2010, she became the youngest artist in history to win the music industry's highest honor, the Grammy Award for Album of the Year. She was 20 years old when she won for her album *Fearless*. Alanis Morissette and Barbra Streisand previously tied for that record; both were 21 when they won.

In 2011, Taylor became the youngest artist ever to be named *Billboard* magazine's Woman of the Year. In making the announcement, *Billboard* editorial director Bill Werde said: "Swift's music and songwriting had transcended all genres of music and at the young age of 21, Taylor has already made a major impact on music and has been an incredible role model for aspiring singers/songwriters and young women everywhere. I look forward to watching her career continue to flourish in the years to come."

Taylor's fame is worldwide. Here she wins a 2012 40 Principales Award in Spain.

Taylor took home one of the most prestigious trophies at the May 2012 Billboard Music Awards: Woman of the Year.

Taylor walks the red carpet at the 2013 Golden Globe Awards.

Chapter 2:
OVERACHIEVER

While much has been made of Taylor's enormous success at such a young age, she's tried to hold her head high and keep doing what she does.

"I'm not concerned with people seeing me in a certain way," she told *The Washington Post* in 2008. "Some people see me as a kid, some people see me as an adult. But I'm seriously not going to complain how anybody sees me, as long as they see me."

Most

The most-purchased album of both 2008 and 2009 was Taylor's *Fearless*. In 2009, she claimed the No. 1 and No. 2 positions atop Nielsen's Broadcast Data Systems (BDS) Top 10 Most Played Songs chart (all genres), with "You Belong With Me" and "Love Story," respectively. She also topped the Top 10 Artist Internet Streams chart with more than 46 million song plays.

Most weeks on the *Billboard* charts? That honor goes to Taylor too. Her self-titled debut album, released in 1996, holds the record for *Billboard's* longest charting album this century, and she is tied with the Beatles and Mariah Carey for *Billboard's* Most Top 20 Debuts.

Taylor also holds the record for the most songs – 11 – from one album on the Billboard Hot 100 Charts at the same time. The super hot album? *Fearless* – the most awarded album in country music history.

Time magazine's annual "TIME 100" issue names the people who most affect our world in the categories of Leaders, Heroes,

Taylor rocks in 2013 with a performance during the 2012 edition of "Dick Clark's Rockin' Eve with Ryan Seacrest."

Chapter 2:
OVERACHIEVER

Artists and Thinkers. Taylor was among 31 women named to the 2010 list; she was joined in the Artists category by individuals including Elton John, Simon Cowell, Neil Patrick Harris and Ashton Kutcher.

Oh, and, in 2012, *Forbes* magazine announced that Miss Swift edged out teen heart-throb Justin Bieber as the highest-earning celebrity under 30, taking in more than $57 million.

One and Only

Need further proof that Taylor's in a class of her own? She's the only female artist ever to have five consecutive Top 10 singles from a debut album on the *Billboard* country chart.

She's also the first female solo artist in country music history to write or co-write every song on a platinum-selling debut CD.

In 2008, she became the first musician ever to be honored at the Annual Young Hollywood Awards with the prestigious "Superstar of Tomorrow" Award.

Hottest

Maxim, an international men's magazine known for its pictorials featuring popular actresses, singers and female models, named Taylor to its "Hot 100" list for five consecutive years, from 2008 to 2012. Taylor was joined on the 2012 list, intended to highlight the 100 "hottest" women of the year, by fellow country singers Julianne Hough and Kellie Pickler.

Biggest, brightest, youngest, most talented? Indeed.

At stage at Madrid's Palacio de los Deportes, Taylor expresses her gratitude for her 2012 40 Principales Award.

Chapter 3:

RED Hot

Chapter 3:
RED HOT

Red is the color of energy, passion and action.

It's a strong color that evokes a range of seemingly conflicting emotions from love to betrayal. Red is Cupid and the Devil. The color red excites the emotions and motivates us to take action.

Red, the album, is full of energy, passion and action.

It's an album that evokes a range of seemingly conflicting emotions from love to betrayal. Red is Cupid and the Devil. The album *Red* excites the emotions and motivates us to take action.

And so, it appears, Taylor Swift's newest project could not be more appropriately named.

Red is Taylor's fourth studio album. Released Oct. 22, 2012, through Big Machine Records, *Red* sold 1.2 million copies in its first week – the largest sales week for any album in a decade. It was Taylor's second straight album to sell more than 1 million copies in its first week; *Speak*

Taylor performs on *The Today Show* at New York City's Rockefeller Center in 2010.

Heidkam
&DUN

CMT honors Taylor with its 2010 Artist of the Year award.

Chapter 3:
RED HOT

Now, her third album, sold just over 1 million copies when it was released in 2010. According to Nielsen SoundScan, she's the only female artist to have two albums sell more than 1 million copies during their first week of release. *Red* also set a single-week record at iTunes, where it sold 464,000 copies – all in its first week of release.

If you think selling bazillions of downloads and albums is old hat to the blonde superstar, you're wrong. An excited Taylor tweeted to her fans in late October 2012: "They just told me *Red* sold 1.2 million albums first week. How is this real life?! You are UNREAL. I love you so much. Thanks a million ;)"

Five singles were released in the month leading up to *Red's* release.

"Begin Again" and "Red" both cracked the Top 10 of the *Billboard* Hot 100, while "We Are Never Ever Getting Back Together" and "Red" notched the No. 1 and No. 2 spots respectively on the Hot Country Songs chart.

Part of *Red's* appeal may be the passion with which it was created.

"On this particular record I tried to operate from an emotional place," Taylor told *Billboard* magazine just before the album's release. "I made the emotion of the song a priority rather than asking, 'What should we do from a production standpoint, or what works in this genre?' Instead, it was, 'What did that emotion feel like when I wrote the song?' And whatever the answer was determined what the track sounded like and what my

EX-PIRATION

Don't go breaking Taylor Swift's heart. That message has been broadcast loud and clear to most every human being with a set of XY chromosomes.

Taylor's relationships gone-wrong have famously inspired some of her most popular songs. The lyrics of "Dear John," her 2010 single presumed to be about her breakup with singer John Mayer, are downright brutal: Dear John/ I see it all now that you're gone/ Don't you think I was too young to be messed with?/ The girl in the dress cried the whole way home.

Mayer told *Rolling Stone* that "Dear John" "really humiliated" him, and accused Taylor of "cheap songwriting."

Taylor defends the song saying, "I didn't say anything about the person's identity. 'Dear John' is a well-known concept."

She insists her lyrical representation of what's happened in her relationships has been honest and fair.

"Chances are if they're being written about in a way they don't like, it's because they hurt me really badly," she told *Rolling Stone* in October 2012. "Telling a story only works if you have characters in it. I don't think it's mean. I think it's mean to hurt someone in a relationship."

Taylor's most recent (until the next one) break-up inspired song is her mega-hit "We Are Never Ever Getting Back Together."

She says she was writing another song in the studio with Max Martin and Shellback when someone walked in and mentioned he'd heard Taylor and an ex-boyfriend were getting back together.

"That was not the case," Taylor told Digital Spy in late 2012. "After he left I explained the story to Max and said, 'We are never ever getting back together'

John Mayer

Joe Jonas

Jake Gyllenhal

and someone said we should write that. I just grabbed the guitar and it happened very randomly – we wrote the song in 25 minutes."

Taylor isn't one to kiss-and-tell or even break-up-and-tell; more often, she creates lyrics that simply provide hints and clues about spectacular splits. A few of the exes who have undoubtedly inspired hits:

Brandon Borello was the boyfriend who left for college, thus inspiring the song "Tim McGraw."

"Should've Said No" was about an ex-boyfriend who cheated on her. Taylor mentioned in numerous interviews that the boyfriend's first name was Sam. His last name has widely been reported as Armstrong.

Break-ups are hard. Breaking up over the phone? Not okay. That's the message Taylor sent ex-boyfriend Joe Jonas with her song "Forever & Always."

What's worse than breaking up over the phone? Actor Jake Gyllenhaal reportedly broke up with Taylor via text message. Ouch! No wonder "We Are Never Ever Getting Back Together" is said to be about the Oscar-nominee.

Taylor started dating actor Taylor Lautner after they appeared in the movie *Valentine's Day*. They broke up in early 2010. The song, "Back to December" is suspected to be about him.

Taylor's most recent relationships – and subsequent break-ups – were with One Direction bad-boy Harry Styles and Kennedy-heir Conor Kennedy. Fingers crossed that songs about those ill-fated attractions might show up on future Taylor albums.

Taylor Lautner

Harry Styles

Conor Kennedy

vocals were supposed to sound like."

The emotions in *Red's* 16 genre-crossing tracks run the gamut, from desperation to falling in love to jealousy.

The making of *Red* was a two-year process. During the first year, Taylor wrote 30 to 35 songs on her own, and then worked with her go-to producer Nathan Chapman to put finishing touches on the best of them.

"(Then) my label came to me and they said, 'You're done. This record is finished. Congratulations,'" Taylor told Our Country, Yahoo's country music blog, in October 2012. "And I looked at my label head, Scott Borchetta, and I said, 'I just don't think we are. Because I think it's good but I don't think it's different enough. And I don't think we're covering enough new ground here.' Because this is album four. And when you're making album four, you have two choices: You can either do things the way that you have always done them, and then you're forming a pattern of doing things the same way, or you can switch it up and go outside your comfort zone."

Laughs were plentiful during Taylor's 2012 appearance on *The Tonight show with Jay Leno.*

RED: THE CRITICS REACT

Critics love to, well, criticize. Music critics listen to new albums over and over, often finding fault with the very things fans adore. Lyrics that are "romantic" to one listener, for example, come across as "corny" to another.

The thing that makes a critic's opinion different from the average album-buying fan is that the critic generally broadcasts his thoughts to a broad audience via newspaper, magazine, radio or Internet.

Here's a sampling of what critics had to say about Taylor Swift's fourth album, *Red*:

"As she settles into her superstar persona at the age of 22, Swift has made it clear that she is never going to be pigeonholed, and will always strive for relatable transcendence. *Red* is her most interesting full-length to date, but it probably won't be when all is said and done in her career."

- Andrew Hampp and Jason Lipshutz for Billboard.com

***

"Taylor Swift's *Red*, the Grammy winner's fourth album, is a 16-track set that has the singer continuing to step away from her country roots to take on a more rock and pop sound. The album features songs that are big and stadium ready (she has a U2-like moment on album opener, 'State of Grace') and others that are soft and slow. But while *Red* contains its share of winners, many of the songs lack the colorfulness and vitality the album title suggests, leading to an overall letdown. Lyrically and sonically, the album lacks oomph and feeling: It sounds like we've heard it all from her before (check 'Starlight')."

- Mesfin Fekadu for Huffington Post

***

"Overall, *Red* is more delightfully electro-pop than anything Swift has ever put out before (and that includes 2010's *Speak Now*). With its vibrant blend of heartache and happiness, for me it's her best work to date. And that's no game."

- Tyrone S. Reid for Blogcritics.org

***

"*Red* is a big record that reaches for importance and occasionally touches it, filled with well-constructed pop songs Taylor-made for bedroom duets. If 'Everything Has Changed,' a powerful collaboration with British singer Ed Sheeran, or the mandolin-driven romance 'Treacherous,' were automobiles, they'd be parked in an Audi or BMW showroom — sleek, solid and built for comfort. There are no bumps on *Red*. Only clean, perfectly rendered American popular music.

- Randall Roberts for the *Los Angeles Times*

***

"Forget Swift's age (even if she did write 'Tim McGraw,' the best teenage lyric since Rimbaud's 'Drunken Boat,' when she was a freshman in high school), her Forever-21-fresh image, her alleged ideological failings, *Red* is as smart and catchy a collection of tunes as you'll find on the Internet this year. Pardon me if I hear more vitality and verve in her corniest love-story/break-up anthem than in all the adolescent morosity Justin Vernon wrings from his wounded soul."

- Michael Robbins for *Spin*

***

"Red is, with 16 songs, not a perfect album. There are a couple of bland duet ballads, one with Ed Sheeran and the other with Gary Lightbody from the band Snow Patrol. But even in those contexts, it's the guys' vocals that are the more pallid. For all the once and future criticisms of Swift's voice, its very thinness works in her favor: In the ballads, it enhances the images of fragility in the lyrics. In the faster, louder songs, it operates like a rock singer's instrument; think of Neil Young's high-pitched whine or Exene Cervenka's theoretically 'bad' voice in the punk band X. Like all good pop artists, Swift continues to evolve in a manner that challenges her diehard fans while inviting naysayers to give it another listen. For all her accessibility, she merits and holds up to close scrutiny."

- Ken Tucker for NPR

***

"The sheer size of *Red* makes it difficult to consume in just one or two listens. The shortest track runs 3:17, but most push four, or even five, minutes. It gets better with each listen, as one notices the clever nuances — like how 'Holy Ground' is improved because it follows 'The Last Time.' It's tempting to compare her fourth album to Faith Hill's 2002 album *Cry*, but Swift's poppiest album is still rooted in great songwriting. Expect four or five hit country songs before she reloads for album No. 5 in another two years."

- Billy Dukes for Taste of Country

Taylor performs at a 2010 gala celebrating *Time's* 100 Most Influential People in the World.

Chapter 3:
RED HOT

The decision was an easy one for Taylor. She headed back into the studio and stretched herself by collaborating with seven sets of producers, including Max Martin & Shellback (known for their work with Maroon 5, Pink, Kelly Clarkson), Jeff Bhasker (Kanye West, Alicia Keys) and Butch Walker (Weezer, Fall Out Boy). She also worked with guest artists such as Gary Lightbody and Ed Sheeran. It was a chance for Taylor to make music in ways she never had before.

"It's so healthy as an artist to consistently put yourself in a room with people who are so different, style-wise, and so different in the way that they approach music than you are because it teaches you things," she told CMT Insider in October 2012. "It teaches you new tricks."

While the CD's songs range from pop to country to acoustic, they're linked together by the honest, lyrical stories Taylor is able to weave.

"Every song sounds different from every other song, so you have a lot of country, you have a lot of pop, you have a lot of acoustic, you have a lot of really cool loops that these amazing producers have created," she told CMT Insider.

Among tracks on the CD, music reviewers have been most critical of "The Last Time," a collaboration with Snow Patrol's Gary Lightbody. Critics have called it "an outright slog" and "a snoozer." Meanwhile, "Red," "We Are Never Ever Getting Back Together," "All Too Well," "I

Chapter 3:
RED HOT

Knew You Were Trouble" and "Everything Has Changed" have been (almost) universally praised.

Don't expect Taylor to pick a favorite song from the album – she loves them all for different reasons.

"It took me so long to pare down the list, and these are the ones I love the most," she told CMT. "There are lines that I am so stoked for people to discover — like a second line and the bridge. I am so excited to see if people will quote that on their Facebook page and things like that because, to me, the lyrics are the most exciting thing about putting out a new record and hearing what people think about the lyrics.

"But these are honestly the 16 best songs from the last two years of my life, and I am so excited for people to hear them."

> *"Taylor's one of the most inspirational, positive, good-hearted people that I know. I met her when she was 18, and this was before* Fearless *came out. It is absolutely incredible to see somebody so successful and so humble, and I think she's been a big part of me kind of staying in line."*
> — ***Selena Gomez***
> to *Life & Style*, 2013

Red *Tracks at a Glance*

1. "State of Grace." Taylor wrote this rock-inspired song, *Red's* fourth and final promotional single.

2. "Red." This single uses colors to describe the emotional stages of loving and losing a boyfriend.

3. "Treacherous." This song was co-written and co-produced by Dan Wilson, lead singer of the band Semisonic.

4. "I Knew You Were Trouble." A collaboration with Max Martin and Shellback, this song debuted at No. 3 on the Billboard Hot 100, selling more than 416,000 copies in its first week of release.

5. "All Too Well." Taylor co-wrote this song with Liz Rose. She's called the song "the hardest to write on the album."

6. "22." Another collaboration with Max Martin and Shellback, this pop tune succinctly describes life for a twenty-something.

7. "I Almost Do." Written by Taylor and produced by Nathan Chapman, this is the album's most country-esque track.

8. "We Are Never Ever Getting Back Together." Taylor wrote this sassy pop tune with Max Martin and Shellback; it's the first single from the album.

9. "Stay Stay Stay." This mandolin-heavy song tells of a promise to stay with a current boyfriend while badmouthing those who came before him.

10. "The Last Time." This moody duet with Snow Patrol's Gary Lightbody was produced by Jacknife Lee.

11. "Holy Ground." This country rocker was produced by Jeff Bhasker and tells the story of a relationship that ran on

Taylor arrives at the 2010 "All for the Hall" celebration at the Country Music Hall of Fame.

Taylor was named Best Female Country Artist at the 2010 American Music Awards.

"New York time." Any guesses?

12. "Sad Beautiful Tragic." This Nathan Chapman-produced song is an acoustic heartbreaker.

13. "The Lucky One." Jeff Bhasker produced this tune, which tells the story of a starlet who tires of fame and media scrutiny and opts instead for a hermit-like existence.

14. "Everything Has Changed." Ed Sheeran duets with Taylor on this romantic, guitar-driven song.

15. "Starlight." This song about young, crazy love is, perhaps, the most danceable on the CD.

16. "Begin Again." Produced by Nathan Chapman and Dan Huff, this folksy song is the album's second single.

Target Edition Bonus Tracks

"The Moment I Knew." This song tells a sad, real life-inspired tale of the worst birthday party ever.

"Come Back... Be Here." Let this be a lesson about what can happen if you don't follow your own romantic advice.

"Girl at Home." Cheer up. This one of the bounciest break-ups songs of late.

Taylor performs on stage in Auckland, New Zealand in March, 2012.

Chapter 4:

58 Shows, 45 Cities

Chapter 4:
58 SHOWS, 45 CITIES

When most folks say they're "hitting the road," they mean they're headed to grandma's house or, perhaps, they're taking a drive to the beach.

For Taylor Swift, hitting the road takes on a much grander meaning. The fair-skinned singer-songwriter is spending much of 2013 crisscrossing North America on the Red Tour.

Red kicked off March 13, 2013, in Omaha, Neb., and is scheduled to make stops in 45 cities. The dates include shows in nine stadiums: Detroit's Ford Field, Dallas' Cowboys Stadium, Toronto's Rogers Centre, Winnipeg's Investors' Group Field, Vancouver's BC Place Stadium, Pittsburgh's Heinz Field, Philadelphia's Lincoln Financial Field, Foxborough's Gillette Stadium and Chicago's Soldier Field. Singer/songwriter Ed Sheeran, whose duet with Taylor, "Everything Has Changed," reached the No. 1 spot on the iTunes all-genre chart, will be a special guest on all of the shows on

Taylor opened the last dress rehearsal for her 2011 Speak Now Tour as a fundraiser to benefit tornado victims in the Southeastern United States. The sold-out Nashville show raised more than $750,000.00.

Always the fashionista, Taylor turns heads during a shopping trip in New York City.

Taylor looks dazzling as she arrives at *Billboard's* 2011 Women in Music event in New York City.

the tour.

At the end of 2012, Taylor announced she would likely extend the U.S. leg of the tour by another 30 to 40 dates; a European leg is expected after that. The tour is being produced and promoted by The Messina Group (TMG).

"I didn't think I could be any more excited about my *Red* album, but then I start thinking about how I'm going to put the new show together for The Red Tour," Taylor said when announcing the concerts. "I have so many ideas about how to really bring this music to life, and I can't wait to share the new show with all my fans!"

Fans, too, are excited about the show. When tickets for Red's earliest dates went on sale the morning of Nov. 16, 2012, 14 stadium and arena shows were sold-out within minutes. Among the fastest sell-outs: Los Angeles (two arena shows in one minute), Atlanta (two arena shows in five minutes), Washington, D.C. (two arena shows in five minutes), Toronto (stadium

Taylor's Speak Now World Tour wrapped up its North American run with two sold-out shows at New York City's Madison Square Garden.

show in five minutes), Detroit (stadium show in 10 minutes) and Chicago (stadium show in 25 minutes).

Red is Taylor's third concert tour as a headliner.

The Fearless Tour, in support of her sophomore studio album, was her first tour. Fearless kicked off at Roberts Stadium in Evansville, Ind., on April 23, 2009. The tour, which lasted through mid-2010, included 105 shows in North America, Europe, Australia and Asia. Former *American Idol* contestant Kellie Pickler and the country group Gloriana joined Taylor on much of that tour. Along the way, she also performed with guest artists John Mayer, Faith Hill and Katy Perry; Justin Bieber even joined her for two shows in the United Kingdom.

> *"Maybe this makes me sound like a robot, but there is nothing more interesting to me than my career. I feel so lucky to have found something I love so much. I don't have an identity without music. It probably sounds crazy, but I want to do everything I can to keep this precious thing intact."*
> *— Taylor Swift to the* Boston Globe*, 2008*

Taylor's second concert tour, The Speak Now World Tour, kicked off Feb. 9, 2011,

Taylor's Speak Now World Tour ran from February 2011 to March 2012.

Taylor performed two sold-out shows at Washington, D.C.'s Verizon Center as part of her 2011 Speak Now World Tour.

Taylor arrives at the 2011 Academy Of Country Music Awards.

> *"I don't know how to have a normal relationship because I try to act normal and love from a normal place and live a normal life, but there is sort of an abnormal magnifying glass, like telescope lens, on everything that happens. So, I don't know how to do that correctly or anything. I don't really know that much about love, it turns out."*
> – ***Taylor Swift*** *to ABC News, 2012*

and ran through March 18, 2012, with dates in North America, Europe, Australia and Asia. At the end of 2011, the tour placed fifth on *Billboard's* annual list of "The Top 25 Tours," earning $97 million through 89 shows. It placed 24th in *Billboard's* ranking of 2012 concert tours, with another $26 million earned, taking its total to $123 million.

Speak Now played to more than 1.6 million fans, with 111 shows in 19 countries on four continents. It was such a hit that it got its own exhibit at the Country Music Hall of Fame and Museum in Nashville. The exhibit, which ran through much of 2012, included dozens of Taylor's glitzy costumes, instruments, props and even the Juliet balcony in which she soared above the crowd during each performance of the song "Love Story."

Taylor knows audiences have come to expect her shows to be well-orchestrated and action-packed. She's determined to

Taylor pays tribute to Alan Jackson by playing his song, "Where Were You (When the World Stopped Turning)" during the 2011 Nashville Songwriters Hall of Fame induction ceremony.

Chapter 4:
58 SHOWS, 45 CITIES

make each tour special – different from the one before it. Her goal is to continue wowing fans with her creativity and versatility, the whole time remaining true to herself.

"I like for it to be big – as big as possible," she told *Billboard* magazine. "If we can make a show that dazzles people more than the last tour, then I'll have done my job in the right way."

Teams of producers, promoters, musicians, set designers, costumers and makeup artists are involved in the planning of a tour like Red. Ideas are bounced around, refined and then refined some more. Logistics team members are pulled in to make sure sets can be transported and rebuilt as the concert moves from venue to venue. Financial experts become involved to ensure ticket prices can cover payroll as well as costs associated with the venue, promoter and ticket vendors.

The real planning for the Red tour, though, began long before those meetings – back to the days when Taylor was still writing the music for her new album.

"When I write a song, the first thing I think about is, 'Okay, this is a message to a person, what are they gonna think when they hear it?'" she told *Rolling Stone*. "The second thing I think of is, 'Ooh, how are we gonna play this in concert? What's the lighting gonna be like? What costumes are we gonna have?' So the visual part of the story comes to me pretty quickly after I write the song."

Even with all that planning and preparation, Taylor is careful to keep the details surrounding the tour secret.

"...The element of surprise is still really important in a concert and showing scenes and images and visuals that are magical," she said. "I really like to take people to a different world and change things up constantly, never showing them too much of the same thing too many times in a row."

Taylor looks glamorous at the 2011 Billboard Music Awards.

In her short career, Taylor has gained a reputation for her energetic, emotion-packed live performances.

Chapter 4:

58 SHOWS, 45 CITIES

IT ALL ADDS UP FOR TAYLOR

16	The age at which Taylor released her first album.
26 million	The number of albums Taylor has sold in the United States.
75 million	The number of download sales Taylor has had during her career.
3.1 million	The number of copies of *Red* sold in its first two months of release.
223 million	The number of YouTube views of her 2009 video "You Belong With Me."
2	The number of Taylor's albums that have sold more than 1 million copies in a single week.
3	The number of major concert tours Taylor has headlined.
6	The number of Grammys she's won.
23.6 million	Twitter followers.
13	Her lucky number.

Chapter 5:

Entertainer and Businesswoman

Chapter 5:
ENTERTAINER AND BUSINESSWOMAN

When Scott and Andrea Swift gave birth to their first child in 1989, they – like most parents – put considerable thought into their baby's name. They finally settled on Taylor (after singer-songwriter James Taylor) because her mother believed a gender neutral name would help her forge a career in business.

That plan seems to have worked out pretty well.

Sure Taylor can sing, but she's also become a savvy businesswoman along the way. In 2012, she was second only to Britney Spears among the nation's highest-earning female singers (Taylor earned a reported $57 million).

When Taylor's fourth album, *Red*, was released on October 22, 2012, it rocketed to the top of iTunes' Top Albums chart within a mind-blowing 36 minutes. For fans who wanted a CD they could actually hold in their hands, they had a number of buying options from which to choose. They could

Taylor performs during the 2010 MTV Video Music Awards in Los Angeles.

GENEROSITY BECOMES HER

Taylor Swift's fans know she has a big heart but now it's official: She was named the most charitable celebrity of 2012 by the website DoSomething.org.

The Pennsylvania native works tirelessly to help young cancer victims. Among the many charities she supported financially in 2012: the Elton John AIDS Foundation, UNICEF, Oxfam International and Habitat For Humanity. She also made a $4 million donation to the Country Music Hall of Fame Museum.

As if all that wasn't enough, Taylor demonstrated the true spirit of grace and forgiveness when some pranksters joined forces to rig a contest that allowed Facebook voters to determine which school would win a performance from the singer. The mean-spirited campaign was aimed at sending Taylor to perform for students at Horace Mann School for the Deaf and Hard of Hearing in Allston, Mass.

Taylor preempted the pranksters' efforts and made a personal $10,000 donation to the school. The contest's sponsors, Papa John's and Chegg, each matched the amount as did Cover Girl and American Greetings, resulting in a $50,000 donation to the school. Additionally, Taylor has promised that all Horace Mann students will receive free tickets to her next Boston-area concert.

Need further proof that Taylor's the real deal? In December 2012, she became the youngest person to receive the Ripple of Hope Award from the Robert F. Kennedy Center in recognition of her philanthropy.

In presenting the award, Kerry Kennedy said: "Taylor is just the kind of woman we want our daughters to be: authentic and mighty, willing to take a risk and strong enough to walk away."

Taylor is honored at the 2012 Ripple of Hope Gala.

RFK Center President Kerry Kennedy said of Taylor: "Here's a young woman – 22 years old – who has put herself out in the world, and in an incredibly powerful and strong way."

Guitar in hand, Taylor hits the streets of Manhattan in August 2012.

go out just after midnight and buy the 16-track CD at a 24-hour Walgreens or Wal-Mart – or they could wait until morning, when a 22-track edition was available at Target.

For those who craved more than just music, there were even more shopping choices: at Papa John's, you could get a CD and large pizza (in a pizza box emblazoned with Taylor's image) for $22.

If you already had your CD, you could buy a custom pair of *Red*-inspired Keds sneakers for $50. Taylor's relationship with Keds is ongoing and she's now the "face" of the company's girl-oriented advertising campaign.

Corporations have been seeking endorsements from and partnerships with Taylor almost as soon as her first album hit the shelves.

In 2008, for example, the Venus Embrace shaving system named her the brand's "Goddess of Summer." American Greetings announced its exclusive partnership with

Taylor arrives at the 2011 American Music Awards.

Chapter 5:
ENTERTAINER AND BUSINESSWOMAN

the Grammy-winning pop and country music sensation in November 2009. In 2010, the singer signed a deal with Elizabeth Arden to release a range of fragrances that carry her name. A year later, Cover Girl announced that Taylor Swift would be the face of its new make-up line, NatureLuxe.

That businesses ranging from shoe manufacturers to drug stores want to be aligned with a twenty-something singer may not initially appear to make sense. But when you start to learn about Q scores, those decisions seem more logical.

A Q Score (Quotient Score) is the measurement of the appeal of a brand, celebrity or company. The more people like and respect an item or person, the higher the Q Score.

Henry Schafer, executive vice president of the New York-based Q Scores Co.,

> *"I have friends from all fields – people who are in school, actresses and singers. It's surprising how we don't talk shop. You'd think we'd get together and discuss the stresses of fame but we actually just talk about boys like all the other girls. We don't run through each other's scripts or compare set lists."*
> – ***Taylor Swift*** *to the* London Sun, *2013*

Taylor performs at the 2010 Country Music Association Awards.

Taylor hits a high note during her performance at Z100's 2012 Jingle Ball at Madison Square Garden.

IT'S NOT ALL ROSES

At first glance, it may appear that Taylor Swift is living a very charmed life. She is, but she's also experienced failure, disappointment and embarrassment.

Taylor is the first to admit that, despite her mega-fame, she has some self-confidence issues.

"My confidence is easy to shake," she told NPR's *All Things Considered* in 2012. "I am very well aware of all my flaws. I'm aware of all the insecurities that I have. I have a lot of voices in my head constantly telling me I can't do it, you know?"

Like most celebrities, Taylor has her detractors – music fans who think her voice is too thin or her lyrics are too predictable. After a duet with rock-legend Stevie Nicks at the 2010 Grammy Awards, Taylor had criticism hurled at her like grenades. *The Los Angeles Times* called her performance "strikingly bad" while the *Washington Post* labeled it "incredibly wretched."

Taylor admits the harsh comments sting and she acknowledges that nerves got the best of her during that much maligned Grammy performance.

"...Getting up there on stage thousands of times, you're going to have off nights," she said. "And when you have an off night in front of that many people, and it's pointed out in such a public way, yeah, that gets to you."

Fortunately, when life gives her lemons, Taylor makes lemonade in the form of hit songs.

"...I ended up writing a song called 'Mean' about that experience and about this one particular (music critic) who would not get off my case about it. And to stand up at the Grammys two years later and to sing that song and get a standing ovation for it and to win two Grammys for that particular song, I think, was the most gratifying experience I've ever had in my life."

Taylor's 2010 Grammy performance with Stevie Nicks was a bit of a bust.

Sometimes a song is the best revenge. Taylor performs her hit single "Mean" at the 2012 Grammy Awards.

Taylor attends the 2011 launch of her fragrance, Wonderstruck, at Belk Cool Springs Galleria in Franklin, Tenn.

explained to the *New York Times* that Taylor's Q score is 24 – compared to 17 for the average celebrity and 16 for the average female singer.

When polling only females ages 13 to 24, Taylor's Q score is 26 and among children ages 6 to 12, her Q score is an off-the-charts 45.

"She's been remarkable in her ability to retain her above-average appeal," Schafer said.

Ira Mayer, publisher and executive editor at the New York-based *Licensing Letter*, says it's no doubt companies want to partner with Taylor because her appeal is so wide-ranging.

"Even people who don't like country music like her," he said.

> *"I don't really take my clothes off because I don't think I can pull it off. Also, most people are only going to focus on one or two things about you – I want that to be that I write my own songs, not that I have great abs."*
>
> – ***Taylor Swift***
> *to the* London Sun, *2013*

Need further proof?

In January 2013, the Coca-Cola Co. announced it had signed Taylor to a big-time, long-term endorsement deal for its Diet Coke brand. The deal makes

Chapter 5:
ENTERTAINER AND BUSINESSWOMAN

Taylor the centerpiece of Diet Coke's "Stay Extraordinary" campaign and "will be integrated into all key marketing efforts for the brand," including TV, print and digital advertising, according to the company. The partnership puts fans at the forefront of everything Taylor and Diet Coke do together. Diet Coke's social media channels, for example, will serve as a sort of backstage pass for fans. Ongoing videos, photos and updates from Swift will give fans a glimpse into her career and personal life.

"Taylor's unmatched business savvy, talent and drive to succeed are an inspiration to everyone," said Katie Bayne, Coca-Cola Co.'s President of North America Brands. "She's an extraordinary individual and a wonderful symbol of achievement."

Yes, Taylor Swift is America's sweetheart but she's also a clever and experienced business woman. Instead of a manager, she has a management team – which she heads up.

Scott Borchetta, who first signed Taylor to Big Machine Records, describes her as "scary smart."

Plenty of musicians can sing or play the guitar. What sets Taylor apart from the rest? Intelligence and business acumen combined with a healthy dose of girl-next-door relatability. She still gets her heart broken, she still feels lonely and she's never forgotten where she came from – that kind of appeal goes a long, long way with fans.

Taylor's talent and intelligence make her a savvy businesswoman and marketer.

Taylor performs during New Year's Eve in Times Square in New York City on December 31, 2012.

Chapter 6:

Transcending Country Music

Chapter 6:
TRANSCENDING COUNTRY MUSIC

If you're one of those people who like things in neatly labeled packages, you probably don't like Taylor Swift.

She is, after all, a nonconforming, stereotype-defying, rule-breaking, won't-be-pigeonholed, genre-crossing musician if ever there was one. Is she a country star trying to make it in the pop music world? Is she a pop star in a country sheep's clothing?

Taylor's new album, *Red*, has been repeatedly called out – not necessarily in a bad way – for its genre-spanning songs.

The truth is traditional country music isn't all that traditional anymore. Yes, there's still plenty of heartache in the lyrics, there may be a fiddle in the band, and you may hear some twang in the vocals, but most current country artists are taking pride in their ability to stretch their musical muscles.

"I'll stop and play with anybody, anywhere, any kind of music they want to play," "Big" Kenny Alphin, half of the country duo Big & Rich, told the Associated Press in late 2010. "Because

Country? Pop? Rock? Whatever you do, don't try to box Taylor in.

Taylor attends *Time's* 2010 "100 Most Influential People in the World" gala.

Taylor greets fans at a 2010 concert feting country duo Brooks & Dunn.

first and foremost, I'm a musician and a songwriter and I don't need the labels."

Alphin said it's important to recognize and celebrate the cultural diversity of different kinds of music, but musicians should be energized by the opportunity to branch out, try new sounds and bring diverse influences together.

Ricardo Baca, music critic for the *Denver Post*, wrote an article in 2011 explaining that crossing over from one genre to another makes good business sense.

"Appealing to fans of multiple genres helps sell more records, merchandise and tickets and makes a larger imprint along the way," he wrote. But then he went on to say that Taylor "isn't a crossover so much as a crossed-over ... She's more pop culture than pop-country, more spotlight sequins than frilly fringe. Yes, Taylor Swift is more MTV than CMT, more Katy Perry than The Band Perry."

Baca's assessment offended some true-blue Taylor fans. But why? If you love

Taylor speaks to the audience at the 2013 Radio Disney Music Awards via closed-circuit TV.

Chapter 6:
TRANSCENDING COUNTRY MUSIC

Taylor's music, does it matter what section of the music store it's filed under?

Jon Caramanica of the *New York Times*, suggests that, as Taylor's popularity has soared, she's been able to create her own label: "nontransgressive, rose-colored female pop megastar, the likes of which we haven't seen in decades... Country radio no longer gets to define her, and pop music has accepted her novel terms."

Saxophonist Dave Koz, who has performed with artists ranging from rocker Richard Marx and country crooner Toby Keith to jazz fusionist Jeff Lorber, told the Associated Press that the most successful musicians are those who are open to crossing genre boundaries.

> *"I'm a fan of Taylor's, not just her work but her ethics and that she writes her hits herself and she's probably the only woman in her position in the industry who writes 100% of her hits."*
>
> – ***Ed Sheeran***
> *to the* London Daily Star, *2013*

"I think the people who are willing to try and get out of their comfort zone and try new things and experiment and collaborate are the ones who are going to push music

Taylor performs for Australian fans during a 2012 show in Perth.

Taylor poses for the paparazzi as she arrives at the 2013 Golden Globe Awards.

The California launch of her new fragrance was the perfect occasion for Taylor to strike a pose.

to where it really needs to go," he said, noting that allowing music to morph and grow often leads to an improved, more pleasing product.

"When you take the shackles off from having to stay in one genre and following the rule, 'This is what I do and only what I do,' the minute you take all of those blinders off, people start to be much more creative," Koz said.

Four-time Country Music Association Entertainer of the Year Kenny Chesney suggests that pigeonholing music into well-divided categories is an old-fashioned notion.

"I think that my audience listens to more than just country music," he told *Newsday* in Fall 2009.

Chesney's fans proved that to him when he invited rocker Dave Matthews to play with him onstage.

"I said, 'You should come out and do ('Where Are You Going?'), and we'll do a (Bob) Marley song or something,' and he was legitimately scared that my audience wouldn't know who he was," Chesney said. "He walked out onstage, and I introduced him as 'From Charlottesville, Virginia, my friend Dave Matthews,' and the crowd went crazy. You could tell it was a relief off his shoulders. That's when we both knew that they may be listening to a Kenny Chesney record, but they're also listening to a Dave Matthews record. We share an audience of people who just love music."

For her part, Taylor insists she doesn't

LIVE LIKE TAYLOR

Taylor Swift's fashion sense is undeniably whimsical. It's not surprising, then, that her décor style follows suit.

The country superstar bought her luxurious 4,062 square-foot penthouse condo in 2009 for $1.99 million. Actress/singer Hayden Panettiere lives in the same Adelicia complex in downtown Nashville.

Taylor's three-bedroom, four-and-a-half bath home was once an ultramodern bachelor pad. But, thanks to more than a year of remodeling and redecorating, it has been transformed into a contemporary, comfortable and – yes, whimsical showplace.

Her one-of-a-kind home includes a gourmet kitchen, fireplaces, floor-to-ceiling windows and a koi pond – yes, inside her condo. Color is everywhere – on the walls, the ceilings, the fabrics. But the real focal point is the spiral staircase that leads to a wooden, human-size "birdcage" filled with pillows. "It's the most comfortable place in the world," Taylor told *Rolling Stone*.

Building your own over-sized birdcage may be out of the question, but these simple tips will allow you to emulate Taylor's fanciful style in your very own room:

- A muted color palette and lots of mixed patterns will lay the foundation for a boho chic look. Hit secondhand stores and flea markets in a quest for vintage fabrics in a variety of textures. Artwork doesn't need to be spendy; frame an antique handkerchief or pretty, hand-embroidered tea towels. For a touch of sparkle, drape gold chains or beads around lampshades.
- Personalize! Taylor's home includes dozens of photos in ornate gold frames. If you can't find gold frames you love, use metallic spray paint to transform thrift store finds. Add textural interest by gluing trinkets or coins to the frames before painting.
- A cute chandelier can add feminine elegance to your space. Already have a ceiling-mounted fixture? Add crystals, beads or flowery shades to give it romantic flare. If transforming your light is out of the question, take a cue directly from Taylor: Use fish line to hang crystalline stars from the ceiling around it.
- Don't think you have to shop at exclusive boutiques to get fun, trendy décor items. "I love Target and Walmart," Taylor told *In Touch* magazine in 2010. "I find the coolest things there."